Hydroponics:Aquaponics

The Ultimate 2 in 1 Guide to Mastering

Aquaponics and Hydroponics for Beginners!

GW00726046

2 Books in 1

Book # 1 – Aquaponics

Book # 2 – Hydroponics

Book # 1

Aquaponics

*The Ultimate Guide to Growing Vegetables
and Raising Fish with Aquaponic Gardening*

Table of Contents

Introduction

I want to thank you and congratulate you for downloading the book, Aquaponics.

This book contains proven steps and strategies on how to rear fish and grow crops, particularly vegetables, within the same habitat. It identifies the plant and fish species that do best in aquaponic farming.

You will learn how to organically deal with pests and parasitic attacks, and also how to deal with varying pH levels and environmental temperatures. You will also see a list of nutrients that a plant normally requires in order to grow well. This book literally gives you all the information you need to start your own aquaponic farming.

Thanks again for downloading this book, I hope you enjoy it!

Chapter 1

What is Aquaponics?

Does this name sound very scientific, or is it just me? Incidentally, this hi-tech sounding name carries a very simple meaning: utilizing waste from water creatures to grow plants. So, waste from water animals – or more respectful, aquatic animals - becomes food for plants. Aquaponics is actually one of the ways to optimize the resources available to provide food with invaluable nutrients to people.

Of course, there is something unique about the whole process of growing the plants because you do not need earth, as in soil. In short, in this very unique process, the plants grow in water just like fish do; they call it hydroponics. This *hydroponics* also sounds very scientific but at least you know *hydro* is something to do with water; so it will not leave you bewildered.

So this farming technique uses liquid to produce vegetables and suchlike food, just the same way we use water to rear fish. And we are talking of plants that would ordinarily grow on land; the ones referred to as terrestrial plants.

Will any water suffice in aquaponics?

No and yes. Meaning? The water could be from a river, lake or dam, but the most important aspect is the composition of nutrients in that water. Normally you know clean water has just a few minerals that include mainly hydrogen and oxygen, as in H_2O, and those are, obviously, insufficient to grow your vegetables from tender seedlings to the dining table. So, clearly, the water used in aquaponics needs to be richer. And that is where animal refuse comes in.

How animal farming helps in plant farming

Aquaponic lies in between aquaculture and hydroponics. And remember we mentioned that aquaponics utilizes animal refuse as plant food. Now, if you notice, aquaponics and aquaculture have a similar beginning. The aqua part indicates that both deal with water or liquid material. Aquaculture nurtures both water living animals and water living plants in order to produce food; and its geographical zone is broad and varied - including wild habitat like ocean and sea coastal areas. Hydroponics, on its part, deals solely with nurturing of plants in a watery environment that could sometimes have sand or gravel; still for the purpose of producing food. Now the place of mutual benefit is what we are calling aquaponics.

Why marry aquaculture and hydroponics to get aquaponics?

As mentioned above, this is an issue of optimizing the available resources. It is important to keep the cost of production as low as possible if we are to feed the world adequately and in a healthy way.

For example, in hydroponics, it takes a big wallet to be able to supply the plants with all the necessary nutrients. In any case, you have got to buy them. Incidentally, these nutrients can go up to 20 in number, and the only ones that you do not need to buy are the ones that the natural water provides; namely, oxygen, hydrogen and carbon. Just think of the following nutrients that you need to enrich your water when doing hydroponics:

Macronutrients	Micronutrients (Essential Trace Elements)	Other useful minerals
Nitrogen	Chloride	Cobalt
Phosphorus	Copper	Silicon
Potassium	Boron	
Calcium	Iron	
Magnesium	Manganese	
Sulphur	Sodium	
	Zinc	
	Nickel	
	Molybdenum	

Then again, you cannot go on pumping sodium, phosphorous, copper, potassium, chloride, zinc, and all those other nutrients endlessly, and expect the environment to remain still healthy for the plants. Not with the whole process of food synthesis and release of by products by the plants. So, understandably, there is need to periodically flush the systems in order to dispose of waste. These processes not only call for consistent injection of money into the project, but also time.

Then there are the challenges on the part on aquaculture. This one now calls for daily attention: clearing some portions of water as a way of dealing with excess nutrients in the liquid. This is not cheap either, especially when it comes to labor and supply of water; hence, the logic in merging the two farming technologies.

So how, exactly, does aquaponics cost you less to farm?

Here it is. You have your fish in the usual place: tank, pond or such other place. As life continues, the fish are feeding and relieving themselves, because you obviously supply them with food. Do you know what would happen if that water remained intact for long? You would soon lose your fish due to toxicity. But in aquaponics, you have an outlet from your fish habitat, which carries the water with fish refuse to the plants' hydroponic tray. The plants flourish from the richness of that water, and as they consume the nutrients, the water becomes cleaner. That water is soon clean enough for the fish to dwell in; and, at that juncture, it is let back into the fish dwelling. So, in aquaponics, the fish benefit the plants and the plants benefit the fish – all to your advantage.

Chapter 2

What Vegetables and Fish Do Well In Aquaponics?

Ever had a waiter come to your table to ask what you preferred to have, without any concern that there was no menu within site? Funny, it appears; but it does happen. Here, we do not want to do the same, leaving you to imagine what you could grow even with no idea what is possible and what is not.

Here are some plants that do well in aquaponics:

A.   These plants grow easily and conveniently using aquaponics.

Type of Plant	Type of Plant
Leafy lettuce of any kind	Chives
Kale	Watercress
Swiss Chard	Mint
Basil	Pak Choi
Arugula	Many other house plants

B.   Other plants that grow in aquaponics but demand an extra rich environment:

Type of Plant	Type of Plant

Tomatoes	Pepper
Cucumber	Beans
Peas	Squash
Broccoli	Cauliflower
Cabbage	

Considering how important vegetables and beans are in terms of nutrients required for good health, aquaponics is, definitely, a technique you would want to know.

And as usual, agricultural scientists are always experimenting, not only to upgrade plant and animal species, but also to see what different species will survive in different environments. In that regard, let us look at a group of plants that big firms like Nelson and Pade, Inc. have managed to grow using cost-effective method:

C.

Type of Plant	Type of Plant
Bananas	Onions
Sweet Corn	Beets
Micro Greens	Carrots
Radishes	Lemon

Lime	Oranges
Orchids	Violas
Nasturtium	Dwarf Pomegranate Tree

D.

In Aquaponics both the fish and the plants are equally important. Before we look at the specifics of the fish/plant relationship, let us look at the species of fish that have been tried in aquaponics and done exemplary well.

Fish Species	Fish Species
Tilapia	Pacu
Sunfish	Koi
Fancy Goldfish	Crappie
Blue Gill	Angelfish
Guppies	Tetras
Swordfish	Mollies
Many other ornamental fish	

E. Agriculture is an ever improving sector and, through aquaponics, other not-so-common fish have been bred and reared.

Below are some of them:

Fish Species	Fish Species
Barramundi	Carp
Yellow Perch	Catfish
Large Mouth Bass	Golden Perch
Silver Perch	

Chapter 3

Is an Aquaponic System Pest Free?

Surely no part of the world lacks irritants. Even the market with all its mirthful chatter has its mad man (or woman). So even the plants you are trying to grow will sometimes have a caterpillar here and there, or some of those parasitic elements like fungi. The good part of aquaponics is that you can solve most of these pest issues organically. So your fish remain safe from toxicity, and your consumers' health is protected too.

Here is how you can deal with pests in aquaponics:

A. Plants

a   Caterpillars

When you see these wiggling or crawling creatures trying to sample your plants like they were connoisseurs of sorts, all you need is this soil borne bacteria that is entirely natural, and you apply it. You can buy it in various outlets that specialize in aquaponic related products; often labeled *organic*. This category of bacteria is known as *Bacillus thuringiensis* and it is sold in form of a spray.

b   Insect which suck plant sap

These are particularly dangerous because sucking sap from your plants is like draining life out of them. So you need to ensure those pests are nowhere within your plant area. This, you do, by spraying natural pesticides like garlic based sprays. And do not for a moment think that chilli is only hot on your tongue; it is also used, in form of a spray, to burn off those pests. But note: moderation is it − do not overspray your plants. Like everything else, an overdose is never helpful.

c Mould and fungi

These are parasites that can mess up your farming if you are not keen. But, of course, you cannot be an aquaponic farmer and not be serious. So you will, obviously, note the onset of a fungal attack and address it fast. All you need is a spray that is based on Potassium bicarbonate and your plants are safe.

All these sprays are available commercially; just check that you do not buy from quacks; buy from credible vendors and note the writings on the label to ensure you are dealing with organic stuff.

d Slugs

How have heard of men (rarely women − I think) who have been drugged and robbed? Or let us say overfed with booze and then robbed and ditched someplace? A terrible thing to happen to anyone: but it is recommended you do that to slugs if they prove to be irritants in your farming endeavor. And how do you do that? That is fun: find a small saucer. Fill it in with beer − it does not have to be your favorite brand, of course. Some cheap stuff from down the street alley will do. Place the beer-filled saucer somewhere around the plants. These not-so-appealing creatures will crawl to the saucer; apparently the smell attracts them. After that, no other science is required: they just drown, and your problem is gone.

e Other irritants like aphids; thrips; and whiteflies

Strategically lay out some sticky straps that are colored. These pests will just stick on them as they move in targeting your plants.

Among the advantages of aquaponics is the room you have for DIY (Do It Yourself). It makes crop management relatively cheap.

B.   Fish

Fish, too, are not without enemies; only, like plants, their enemies are manageable. If you ever have a problem with your fish, it will usually be due to one or more of these situations:

a) Ammonia Toxicity

How do you know the environment if toxic in this way?

As is expected, you are an observant farmer. So you will notice:

- Your fish seem lethargic
- They have visible red streaks on their body; sometimes on their fins
- They seem to be gasping for breath
- Their gills are red; in fact, inflamed.
- Their appetite is down

b) Fungal infection

You will easily see that your fish have this fungal attack by just looking at them. Here are the signs:

- White botches on the bodies of the fish

- White botches on their fins

c) Low level of oxygen in the water

This situation is a case of dissolved oxygen being lower than it is necessary for the survival of your fish. Here is how to know there is trouble:

- Fish begin to drop dead, one after another

- You see your fish struggling to breath

- As the weather turns hot, you realize your fish are dying even faster

- In the morning, you realize you have overnight fish fatalities

- You can see algae in your pond, fish tank or whatever fish rearing facility you are using

How do you deal with natural attacks on fish?

Well, the best and simplest way to avoid the problems of disease is rearing a species that is hardy; fish that is not prone to disease, and fish that is not prone to pests. This is because most diseases may call for curative measures that require chemical medicines, which is something you would like to avoid for a number of good reasons. These reasons include:

i) You can authoritatively tell buyers that your fish are strictly organically reared. And that, in addition to guaranteed market, is bound to raise your price a notch higher.

ii) You do not want to use chemicals that are likely to be in the fish even as you eat it.

But if you are really pressed, you can go for Potassium bicarbonate, which is a natural fungicide. It is eco-friendly and its label as you buy it should indicate that.

What are some of the hardy fish species?

You will be right to talk of these two fish species as hardy when it comes to disease:

- Jade Perch
- Silver Perch

Chapter 4

Did you know that fish can suffer stress and die?

First of all let us admit that it would be sad to lose fish when using aquaponics because that would be tantamount to losing the plants as well; of course, due to the inter-dependence. Secondly, it is costly to counter the effects of stress on fish, because, as in human beings, stress drags along other ailments, some which are fatal.

This is how you deal with situations that stress your fish:

Stressful Situation	How the stressful situation is	Solution
Shortage of oxygen in the water	This is the situation that gets your fish gasping for breath; and sometimes dying	• Aerate the water mechanically • Simply introduce an aerator
Excess solids in the water	In this situation, solids, mostly from excretion, accumulate and begin to raise the level of ammonia in the water. This high concentration of	• Ensure more clean water is being pumped into the fish dwelling, possibly by having a branch from the main pump lead back to improve water circulation. In any

	ammonia causes oxygen levels to fall. So the fish can get ill or just begin to drop dead.	case, with proper and continuous circulation of water, the solids are bound to float, making it easy to remove them.
Excessive nutrients	Usually, the culprit here is ammonia. The breaking down of the protein part of the fish feed serves to increase ammonia in the water. Also rising temperatures and rising pH levels increase the generation of ammonia. And once the ammonia level is too high, your fish are in danger of death.	• Add lemon juice to lower the water pH. • Reduce the fish food rations, even as you speed up the entry of fresh water into the fish dwelling. • You could remove some fish thus reducing refuse and, hence, ammonia.
Origin of water	If you have water that is too chlorinated, like that	• Dechlorinate the water before allowing it in the fish area.

	one that is distributed in many cities, your fish will be in trouble.	• Otherwise, stick to tank water, which is relatively safe.
Algae	Algae raise your water pH. In addition the science of how algae releases oxygen into the water is not fish friendly; a lot of oxygen in the day and none at night.	• Get rid of algae from the water. • Get rid of sunlight from your fish tank; this will make it unfavorable for algae. To do this, you can paint your tank. Also in building your tank, you can decide to use impervious material for the tank walls.

Chapter 5

A Simple Way to Start Off Your Aquaponic Farming

Once you go beyond the scientific and botanical terminologies, which in any case are relatively few in this area, you will be able to embark on your aquaponic farming with minimal assistance. We need to begin by looking at the available options of aquaponic farming systems and their benefits.

Different Aquaponic Systems and Their Advantages

Farmers are not homogenous; fish are not; and even plants are not. So, it is a good idea to be able to choose how to rear your fish as an individual, and also how to go about manning your plants. For that reason, we shall analyze the major systems of aquaponics in use, and you can then take advantage of the one that suits your circumstances.

1. Media-filled beds

These are the simplest. For the plant zone, you just get a massive container and fill it with a medium of rock made of expanded clay or something that close. It is the place that you will allow water from the fish dwelling to flood and then you clear it; or even let the water flow continuously.

2. NFT, standing for Nutrient Film Technique

Though not very common, some farmers still opt to use this system. It involves small gutters that are enclosed within the crop farming area, and the nutrient rich water from the fish dwelling flows through in a thin film. Each individual plant stands in a tiny cup made of plastic, and only its roots dip into the water. This method is limited to a great extent in the variety of plants it can handle, and this is simply because of the expanse of the root system. Plants like the leafy greens and plants that are bigger in size may not do well in this system.

3. DWC, standing for Deep Water Culture

Here, you have a place where water from the fish dwelling is flowing into. Then you have plants within a floating raft – possibly a foam raft. The roots of the plants will literally be floating in water and pulling in the rich nutrients as the plants flourish.

Other times, the floating raft where the plants are is simply placed atop the fishing tank. The former technique is, however, more favored by farmers.

So, now, how do you go about establishing your system and proceeding to farm?

1) Identify the media bed that you want

For a beginner, DWC is convenient and relatively easy to use. This is because the media bed does all the important functions at once. This is how it goes:

- Removes mechanical solids by filtering the water

- Mineralization, which is basically breaking down solids and cycling of water

- Biofiltration

2) Decide how big you want your grow bed to be

Whatever size of grow bed you settle on, just have in the mind the standard depth of that area, which is 30cm deep. With such depth, it is unlikely that the roots of any plant will be inhibited by depth. So the plants will absorb enough nutrients to make them healthy.

3) Decide what size of fish tank you want

Even with all the liberty to choose, experts advise that you make 1,000 liters your minimum capacity for your tank. As a beginner, and possibly a layman, they say the bigger the tank, the more room you have to make mistakes and not harm your fish. They estimate that a single fish of 30cm in length is comfortable being within 200 liters of water.

4) Be careful about the ratio of your tank size to Grow area

Consider the volume of the two: Grow bed to fish tank, and begin with a ratio of 1:1. After all, you want to be cautious in everything, especially when you are new to this system of farming. Of course, you will learn more than a few things in the first few months, and in due course, possible within 4mths – 6mths, you will ready to raise the ratio to 2:1.

5) Mind the number of fish

Mark you aquaponics is not a license to imprison fish; they need to be able to swim freely – eating, playing (if they do), and living as near as possible to a natural habitat. The good experts, therefore, provide you with a guideline: equate a 500g fish to a surface area on the Grow bed, of 0.1m².

6) Mind the Water Temperature

To be on the safe side, establish the fish species that adapt well to changing temperatures. If it becomes difficult to acquire those, then you better settle for those that require warm temperatures. This is because it is always easier and cheaper to warm up water than to cool it; using insulation, tank painting, and that kind of stuff.

7) Mind the Water pH

Work towards maintaining water pH of between 6.8 and 7.0 all through your system. This is the range that is ideal for both your fish and your plants.

And what happens, if unluckily, the pH falls below optimum range?

If you measure the pH, as you are wont to regularly, and you find it at 6.6 or below, boldly raise it using reasonable amounts of potassium carbonate or calcium hydroxide. In cases where you find it higher than the acceptable range, lower it using nitric acid; phosphoric acid; or any other acceptable hydroponic acid.

8) Think before you choose your fish species

This is what you need to base your thinking on:

- Do I want this fish for consumption or simply for display?

- How is the temperature of the water I am going to use?

- Am I interested in fish species of the herbivore family; carnivore family; or the omnivore family?

Keep in mind that fingerlings need their different area from mature fish; otherwise the mature ones might eat them up.

Conclusion

Thank you again for downloading this book!

I hope this book was able to help you to appreciate how easy it is to do farming using minimal resources of land and manure. It is also my hope that you would now consider rearing fish and growing vegetables using aquaponics, to boost the health of your family and make some money as well.

The next step is to assess the piece of space that you have and see the scale of aquaponic farming that you can do. It would also be a good idea to refer your family and friends to this book so that they, too, can benefit from the rich information provided on aquaponic farming.

Finally, if you enjoyed this book, please take the time to share your thoughts and post a review on Amazon. It'd be greatly appreciated!

Thank you and good luck!

Book # 1

Hydroponics

The Ultimate Beginners Guide to Mastering

Hydroponics for Life!

Table of Contents

Introduction

I want to thank you and congratulate you for downloading the book, *"Hydroponics - The Ultimate Beginners Guide to Mastering Hydroponics for Life!"*

This book contains proven steps and strategies for mastering the art and ways of hydroponics and understanding how it works!

We will discuss the fundamentals of hydroponics and build a deeper understanding of how the system works. If you ever heard of this alternative way of gardening but the information seems overwhelming, this book is for you!

Moreover, this book will take you from being clueless about hydroponics to being equipped with the right knowledge to develop your very own hydroponic system. You will also learn the various types of hydroponic systems, the terms and components and the plants that can be grown hydroponically. Likewise, we will also discuss the types of mediums you can effectively use, their characteristics and downsides.

If you take the time to read this book fully and apply the information held within this book will help you to efficiently adopt this extremely beneficial gardening technology and grow your own hydroponic garden and reap the benefits of it.

Thanks again for downloading this book, I hope you enjoy it!

Chapter 1

Hydroponics: Going Soilless

Using the hydroponic system in gardening is not a new way of gardening as what most of us think. The ancient people of Babylon and the Aztecs already adopt this system making the Hanging Gardens of Babylon a popular one. In Asia, the Chinese people also incorporated hydroponic system in their Floating Gardens of China. And in India, plants were grown in coconut husks. Hence, hydroponics is not a new technology. However, there are new innovations applied to make this technique more effective enabling us to grow plants faster and healthier. One of which is by studying the hydroponics in space conducted by the government of the United States.

Hydroponics came from the words "Hydro" or water and "ponos" meaning labor or work. Apparently, this system uses water, a growing medium and other components to do all the work in order for the plant to grow. Hydroponics made it possible for plants to grow even without soil.

The method was further proven by William Frederick Gericke. He popularized the idea of planting soilless while he's working at the University of California. Instead of soil, he claimed that the plants can grow using water and a solution of nutrients which his colleagues didn't believe to be possible. Thanks to Gericke's experiment which he later called the method as hydroponics as various researches were further conducted uncovering a myriad of benefits.

The Fundamentals

Building a hydroponic system means developing a new kind of environment where plants can live in. It is vital to know the different variables present in this system to succeed. Likewise, it will also let you optimize them, troubleshoot the problems you may encounter and figure out the possible solutions so things can work in harmony. More than just being aesthetic, a well-designed hydroponic system is a utopia for plants.

While a little light and water can keep the plants alive, more likely the plants won't thrive using only these components. Like humans, plants and animals are made of organic matter and every organic matter is made up of elements such as oxygen, nitrogen, hydrogen and carbon. These elements composed 90% of the plant's weight. Moreover, they serve different functions in the plants various systems.

For the plants to thrive, they basically need oxygen, carbon dioxide, water, light and nutrients. Essentially, removing the soil means removing the plant's source of nutrition. By doing so, we are also removing the medium that retains water. This is where hydroponic nutrients apply which we will discuss further. Nonetheless, hydroponics allows you to take over your plant's environment and grow healthier plants faster using various mediums.

What Can You Grow Hydroponically?

Almost any plants can be grown in hydroponic systems but for beginners, it is advisable to start with the small types. Vegetables and herbs grow quickly and easily so you may consider them. Moreover, they only require less maintenance and do not need special type of nutrients. Choose to start with fast-growing plants and maintenance-free plants to evaluate the efficiency of your system. Thus, you can learn how your system works and what needs to be improved. For starters, the best choices would be strawberries, tomatoes, lettuce, spinach and hot peppers. Herbs such as Aloe Vera and oregano do not require huge space and do not expands.

If you are ready for other varieties of plants, make sure that they require similar nutrients so they can grow together. In choosing the type of plant to grow, consider the available space. Avoid large plants such as watermelon and squash if you don't have bigger space to grow them. Likewise, ensure that your hydroponic system is adequate enough to accommodate the plants you choose.

Now, you already have an idea on what is hydroponics. To sum it up, the water culture or hydroponics is the soilless way of growing plants and utilizing the power of water. We'll get to know the advantages of this system in gardening and how it is actually healthier for the plants.

Chapter 2

Components and Terminologies

Learning and mastering hydroponics can be overwhelming especially with all the terms you may encounter in the long run. There is usually too much information making it difficult for beginners to determine a solid base where they can start. Let's discuss these terms as simple as possible.

NUTRIENT SOLUTION

This is probably the most vital part of any hydroponic system. While it may sound complicated, this is basically nutrients dissolved in water which made hydroponics a successful method of growing plants. It just not feed the plants with water but with nutrient-rich water that is essential for the plant's optimal growth. It can be in a form of soluble or in various mixes. We will go into details about nutrient solution as we proceed.

Most of the hydroponics systems keep the nutrient reservoir separate from the grow tray or chamber. For the plant to access the nutrient solution, the delivery system should be working efficiently to move the nutrient solution from its reservoir to the tray and drain the excess back to the reservoir.

NUTRIENT RESERVOIR

Also called as reservoir, holds the nutrient solution before feeding the plants. It can be a large container made of plastic and an old fish tank that can hold plenty of water. Keep in mind that the reservoir should not be made of metallic materials to avoid harmful elements to mix with the nutrient solution.

GROWING MEDIUM

Basically, this is where you are letting your plant grows. In soil gardening, soil is the medium used and in hydroponics, various materials can be used to support the root systems and weight of the plants. We'll discuss more of this on the next chapters.

SUBMERSIBLE PUMP

A submersible pump or "pump" is feature in all hydroponics systems. This is often the same type of pump included in a normal aquarium set-up. It pumps the nutrient water from the reservoir to the grow tray. Aside from keeping the water oxygenated, it also discourages the growth of algae. The submersible pump comes in various shapes and sizes and is widely available in home improvement shops.

TIMER

Depending on the system you will use and its place in the garden, a simple set of timer is essential. You will need this in setting the time of your artificial grow light to control the lighting system. For hydroponic systems such as aeroponic, drip and ebb and flow, a time is essential in controlling the submersible pump.

AIR STONE

Whilst this is not an essential composition of a hydroponic system, an air stone is highly recommended to use. It is ideal in adding oxygen to the nutrient solution. It promotes faster growth of the plants and keeps the solution fresher.

AIR PUMP

This is optional in other hydroponic systems aside deep water culture system. Using an air pump is beneficial and relatively cheap. It helps in supplying oxygen and air in the water.

In deep water culture systems, the air pumps prevent the plants from suffocation while they are drenched with the nutrient solution. For other types of systems, it aids in increasing the level of dissolved oxygen. It keeps the water oxygenated by producing air bubbles. It also enables circulation of the nutrients and helps in reducing pathogens.

GROWING TRAY OR CHAMBER

This will hold the entire plant especially the root zone. It can be made of plastic materials, a container, an old huge tray or anything that can keep your growing plants and provides support. You can use almost any containers for the grow chamber but avoid anything that is made of metal as it may have negative reactions with the nutrient solution.

The container should be filled with plenty of holes for a better flow of water. Apparently, the size of the grow tray will depend on the size and type of hydroponic system you will be using and the plants you will be growing. Bigger plants have huge root systems so they need bigger space to hold them.

GROW LIGHT

A supplemental light is highly required for an indoor hydroponic grow box. The plant needs 10-12 hours of light daily for optimal growth. Set the light hanging over the top of your plants with a distance of about 6 inches from the top point of it. Adjust the lights as your plant gets taller to avoid damaging or burning the leaves. Prolonged light exposure can also damage the roots and gives heat stress to the plants.

As a beginner, you can do a homemade hydroponic system using the resources at home. Search for system plans online and find alternatives to the materials needed instead of purchasing the entire set. You must also consider the space of your grow area, the holding tank or reservoir and room overhead for the lighting system. Start by planting veggies or herbs which are easier to manage to test the efficiency of your system. Make changes or adapt new strategies to become a successful grower.

Chapter 3

Various Types of Hydroponics System

Hydroponic systems allow the plants to grow while inside the place. Here you have full control every areas of the growing cycle. You can control the light and set the temperature levels. Likewise, you can manipulate the vital minerals and the soil is not needed. And because you can provide the plants the necessary nutrients, they are most likely to grow faster versus the traditional planting methods.

Below are various hydroponic systems which are all based on this core idea. Understanding how each type of the system works will help you decide what type of system is suitable for you.

DEEP WATER CULTURE SYSTEM- is composed of a nutrient solution, a tank, an air pump, an air stone and a float that will hold the containers where you will be placing the plants. This system is popular in growing spinach and lettuce since they require larger amount of water. Moreover, this is an inexpensive system that is ideal for personal consumption.

Usually it is composed of large buckets and is usually called as bucket systems. Plants are held using net pots with clay pebbles. You can first root the plants in peat plugs as clones or seedlings and transfer them in the net pots. Growers opt to compromise their water culture system with multiple buckets connected by hoses. The main reservoir which holds the nutrient solution is circled back by the hoses. A submersible pump with timer will fill the buckets with nutrients and water nourishing the root systems inside the bucket. One the pump stops, the solutions will drain back to the reservoir and will be recycled for the next feeding.

WICK SYSTEM- this is the most popular, most inexpensive and easiest system you can build at home. You only need wicking material such as fibrous material or cotton rope as long as it is absorbent. This will enable the nutrient solution to move. This system is ideal for beginners as it does not include moving parts. However, this should only be used in smaller types of plants which do not need much moisture or nutrients. The wick is not capable of supplying large quantities of these elements and large plants may only consume the nutrient solution faster.

EBB AND FLOW/FLOOD AND DRAIN SYSTEM- this works by temporarily flooding the tank with the nutrient solution. You will need submersible pump and two tanks, one for the nutrient solution and the other for the plant. There should be an overflow drain coming from the plant tank back to the solution tank. This is probably one of the easiest systems to use since all its parts and functions are very straightforward. The idea is to flood the system with water that is rich in nutrient and drain it quickly.

You can use either a simple table or a tray to hold the plants. The reservoir normally sits beneath where the water will be pumped into the tray and drained back in the reservoir. You can reuse the water or drained it into waste. Most likely growers recycle the nutrient solution before replacing it.

In this system, you can also utilize several grow mediums to house the growing plants. Among the most popular are the netted pots as its open bottoms and sides allow easy draining. Once drained, the roots have plenty of air that supplies oxygen. Depending on the growth of your plants, you can flood the tray up to three times per day.

DRIP SYSTEM- is one of the most used types among other hydroponic system by indoor growers. It contrasts the idea of flood ebb and flow system by enabling the growers to control the right dose of nutrient solution per plant site. It comes with an output volume allowing the growers to calculate the time of feeding at a specific rate. In this system, the emitters are more likely set to a very slow water flow. The grow tray will drain the solution while an air stone and an air pump will recover the nutrient solution back to its reservoir.

NUTRIENT FILM TECHNIQUE SYSTEM (NFT)- is continuous flow system and is popular in indoor horticulture. The grow pots with plants are usually placed in a channel or a pipe. Here the nutrient solution can be reused or totally drained to waste. However, this system won't allow growers to determine a feeding schedule. It doesn't have timer but instead, the nutrient solution is pumped in a continuous cycle from the reservoir to the grow tray. The good thing about this system is that it only requires minimum maintenance- from the preparation of the nutrient solution to turning the pump on. An air stone is vital to keep the water oxygenated.

And because the root systems are not totally immersed with water, there is lesser possibility of smothering and drowning. The running water that gets past the root systems carries the necessary oxygen molecules for the plants which made them very compact. While the root zones' top sections breathe, the bottom sections are soaked into the nutrient solution. It is important to remember that in any hydroponic system that you choose, air is more needed than water. This is usually the mistake of beginners. Inadequate oxygen in the roots as well as the browning of it is not a good sign for the plants.

AEROPONIC SYSTEM- is the most high-tech and recent type of hydroponic system. Air is mostly the growing medium thus the roots were hanging in the air and were misted as needed to make sure that they receive adequate food to grow. However, loss of power or any scenario that will shut the spraying cycle can make the plants die since the roots of it are "hanging out" to dry.

In this system, the nutrient solution is pumped in a tube while the second pump with greater pressure sprays it as a mist over the roots. However, the misting should be done more frequently as it only offers less food for the plants compared with other system such as the drip system. Hence, a timer which is more advanced is required.

Moreover, the water in this system is more hydrogenated compared with other systems because of the regular and more frequent feedings. The nutrient solution moves around more often which promotes faster growth of the plants.

AQUAPONICS- from the term itself, this system incorporate live aquatic species, creating an ecosystem that is both beneficial for the plants and aquatic life. The nutrient reservoir will serve as habitat for the fishes. The fishes create natural fertilizers for the plants by changing the bacteria into nitrate.

The excrement of the fish releases ammonia which is harmful for them this is why they need to be kept in the nutrient reservoir. When the ammonia mixes with bacteria in the water, it will become nitrate which promotes growth for the plants. In return, the plants will remove the toxins while absorbing the nutrients. When it is already free from ammonia, the water will drain back to the reservoir where the fishes are.

Choosing the hydroponic system to use depends on how much you are going to spend, the kind of plants you wanted to grow and the other resources you will need. Hence, it is vital to choose the one that will match your needs, budget and experience.

Chapter 4

Understanding the Hydroponic Nutrients

Planting soilless would also mean that we are missing out plenty of nutrients that soil has to offer. Hence, hydroponic nutrients are essential to keep the plants growing healthy and fast. The solution aims to replace all the micro and macro nutrients found in the soil.

THE N-P-K RATIO

The N-P-K ratio or Nitrogen/Phosphorus/Potassium ratio is the first thing to notice when browsing nutrient bottles. These 3 numbers are printed in front of each bottle. The NPK ratio tells the exact amount of the macro nutrients each bottle contains. If you see 10-10-10, it means the bottle contains 10% Nitrogen, 10% Phosphorus and 10% Potassium. This ratio adds up to 30% thus, the other 70% of the solution is composed of other micro nutrients, chelating agents and water. The ratio depends on the phase growth of your plants.

The nutrients usually come in two varieties- liquid and powdered. The liquid variant is more popular as it is easier to use compared with the powdered form. However, they are highly concentrated so make sure not to spill on the plants or in any of your body. Most of this variant comes with pH buffers wherein the nutrients will balance the pH of the water for you.

On the other hand, the powdered variety is difficult to fully dissolve in water. Likewise, most of it does not contain pH buffers. Just mixed these nutrient varieties with water and you are set!

THE MACRO NUTRIENTS

Macro nutrients refer to those that are absorbed largely by plants. These nutrients are very important in the plant's growth and development. The nitrogen is essential for the formation of co-enzymes, amino acids and chlorophyll. The phosphorus on the other hand, is necessary for the production of phosphate, sugar and energy. It helps in producing fruits and flowers and encourages root growth as well. Lastly, the potassium is needed for protein synthesis. It aids in manufacturing starches and sugar and provides root growth and hardiness.

Make sure that you will only use the nutrients designed for the hydroponic systems. The nutrients made for soil gardening may contain or lack other components and elements. Likewise, ensure that the root zones are only within 68-70 degrees in temperature. Keep the nutrient temp as close to it to avoid problems like damaged fruits, falling off of flowers and stunt growth.

Chapter 5

The "Growing" Medium

Whilst hydroponics means soilless way of growing plants, there are still media to be used in supporting the plants. In most systems, growers opt to use various types of "growing" medium that will support the roots of the plants and sustain the oxygen and water ratio. Getting the right medium is as important as acquiring the right hydroponic system.

In choosing the growing medium, consider the absorption it can provide and the support to keep the plants upright. The medium will greatly affect the amount of oxygen and nutrients your plants receive thus, it has a great impact on the plant's growth rates.

THINGS TO CONSIDER

Before purchasing or setting the medium you will use, ask yourself first; will this medium be able to release adequate nutrients and oxygen? How well the medium can absorb the nutrients plays a huge, vital role in the plant's quality of yield and growth.

Likewise, you would want the growing medium to maintain oxygen which the plants need to grow. See to it that the medium can retain oxygen even when drench with water and nutrient solution. Moreover, the medium's capability to maintain water is important. There are mediums that are able to absorb water and keep it for longer.

Unfortunately, we cannot really say whether a medium is perfect or not. Various types of hydroponics systems can work better with some growing mediums compared to others. Hence, to determine the growing medium to use, consider first the type of hydroponic system you will use which is base on the plant you want to grow.

Certain plants would grow better and faster in a specific type of materials. Moreover, several types of systems work better in certain mediums. Below are some of the most common types of mediums you can use. Use this guide in determining the suitable medium for you.

ROCKWOOL- is an extremely effective medium that has become popular for growers in recent years. It is primarily composed of melted limestone and granite. It is usually available in cubes that are perfect for beginners but even commercialized and huge industrialized farms opt to use it.

This medium is efficient since it has an exceptional ability to hold oxygen and water. It offers the roots the incessant access to greater amount of oxygen and prevents dehydration of the plants. However, rock wool is known to be harmful to the skin and the lungs so be careful when using it. Its small fibers and dust can lodge into the lungs. To avoid this, immediately soak the rock wool in water after taking it out from its package.

Moreover, it is best to use with ebb-and flow, nutrients-film technique, drip and deep water culture systems and in contrast with aquaponic system.

VERMICULITE- this is a mined mineral. Vermiculite is subject to extreme heat making it expand before you can use it as a medium. It is normally used with another growing medium called as perlite as they complement each other very well. It has the ability to sustain moisture while perlite does the opposite. However, you cannot use the vermiculite solely as it tends to hold too much water thus, drowning the plants.

A mixture of perlite and vermiculite (75-25) is ideal or an equal ratio of 50-50. Since this material is very lightweight, it is not advisable to use with the ebb-and-flow system or it will be washed away. It is best to use in aeroponic and drip systems.

PERLITE- is also a mineral and similar with vermiculite, it should be exposed to extreme heat before it can be used a medium. Likewise, it is one of the most inexpensive medium and has the ability to retain oxygen and nutrients longer. However, the biggest downside of it is that it easily loses moisture which is why growers opt to use it with vermiculite, coco coir and soil.

Moreover, this is not advisable to use with the ebb-and-flow system since it is very lightweight and porous that can be easily wash away during flooding. Likewise, this medium is ideal for growing long-term crops but make sure that there is no moisture deficiency which is the usual problem in using perlite.

GROW ROCK- essentially; these are clay pellets that were exposed to intense heat causing the clay to expand. The process leaves the clay with plenty of air pockets which makes it ideal in retaining oxygen. However, grow rocks cannot retain water efficiently. Growers use other moisture-retaining mediums and compounds in conjunction to grow rocks. Coconut fiber is the most common partner of grow rocks and scientists even consider them the best possible combination of growing medium. The downside is that grow rocks are quiet expensive but they can be reused for a longer period and is ideal for ebb-andoflow and aquaponic systems.

COCO▢UT▢▢▢▢ER▢COCO▢OIR- shares the same popularity with rock wool. It has all the advantages of the rock wool but performs better in terms of oxygen and water retention. Moreover, it is completely organic (a by-product of coconut farming) compare to rock wool that is known to be health hazard.

The coco coir is made from the coconut husk which makes it an ideal growing medium. The husk will protect the plants and is good for germination. Plus, it promotes great air to water ratio so the roots will not drown.

However, the market also sells lesser quality coconut fiber products so make sure that you are getting the good ones. A low quality coconut fiber has excessive quantity of salt which can damage the plants. It is usually used with growing rocks and recommended for ebb and flow, drip and aquaponic systems.

AIR-in most systems, the growing medium should be filled deeply so that the roots would be entirely submerged but in some systems such as the aeroponic system, the roots hang freely, enabling its access to nutrient solution. Air as a growing medium is recommended to use in deep water culture system and nutrient-film technique system.

O▢▢▢▢CU▢E▢ are similar to rock wool but is more effective in terms of seedling and germination. It works similarly with the green foam-like material you usually see where flowers are embedded. Moreover, it is inexpensive and do not require pre-soaking. However, the downsides of oasis cubes are being inorganic and are only ideal for germination but not as growing medium for full-term plants.

☐T☐RTER☐☐LU☐☐ also known as the sponge start, starter plugs are the newest hydroponic media space introduced. The good thing about is that it's made from organic compost. Because of the biodegradable binding elements, it doesn't break apart.

It is also ideal to use in growing seeds and clones before introducing them to your hydroponic system. Starter plugs are relatively sustainable and is a good medium to grow large quantities of plants. The roots will grow straight downward making it easier for you to transplant them in the system. The downside is, it is expensive and is only ideal for cloning or starting seeds. They are also prone with fungus gnats which can affect the plants.

RICE☐☐ULL☐ are the shells of the rice grain. Like the coco fiber and coco coir, rice hulls are the by-products that would normally turn to waste so growers opt to re-purpose them by using them in their hydroponics system. However, this medium is not yet that popular since it can only hold little water and decays over time.

☐R☐VEL- this material is usually used in aquariums. Any type of it, as long as it's carefully washed can be use. Gravel is easier to clean, readily available and relatively cheap thus, it is a great starter medium for beginners. It also has the ability to drain well however, certain plant's roots may dry out especially the heavy types. When working with it, make sure that it will not get in contact with water as it may result to pH swings.

PUMICE- is another lightweight mineral similar to perlite. It is capable of retaining high level of oxygen but does not work well with ebb and flow systems.

SAND- is the most abundant among these mediums and extremely cheap or for free. It is ideal for beginners but require frequent sterilization. Moreover, it is also heavy when wet and has poor water retention ability. Certain hydroponic systems are also not compatible with sand.

WOOD FIBER- is an efficient growing medium for hydroponics. Entirely organic, wood fiber is also said to reduce growth regulators which means, larger plants than the usual. The main downside of it is that it is prone to pests which can harm the plants.

POLYSTYRENE PACKING PEANUTS- are the usual packing peanuts that are available everywhere. It is cheap and drains fairly well. Moreover, this is typically used in Nutrient Film Technique system but there is a greater possibility of contamination as the plants can absorb the styrene.

BRICK SHARDS- or crushed bricks work similarly with gravel. These do not have neutral pH so it may affect the water's pH level. And due to the brick dust, it requires frequent thorough cleaning.

Keep in mind that it is impossible to find out what is the best growing mediums as every type of hydroponics systems and plants require different characteristics and abilities. Hence, having an understanding of each type of medium will help you decide wisely on what to use.

Chapter 6

Hydroponic Tips- A Short List

Here is a short list of the things you must keep in mind in hydroponics gardening.

Determine the right equipment to use and how to use it.

Find out the nutritional nutrients your plant needs. Seek help from online communities and forums regarding hydroponics.

Find out the lighting requirements of the plant you will growing.

Only use professional and trusted brand and variants of hydroponic nutrient products.

The feeding schedule should be monitored at the onset of gardening.

Acquire all the necessary materials, equipment, tools and nutrients before planting.

Always check your nutrient solution tank everyday and make some adjustments if necessary.

Minimize the nutrient solutions' light exposure.

Change your nutrients and water and clean the tanks, mediums used and the grow chamber every two weeks without harming the plants.

Sterilize and clean the system thoroughly. Check for harboring pests, fungus and other foreign elements inside the system and in the reservoirs.

Only visit your garden after you shower or have change clothes. Avoid visiting it immediately when you came outdoors to avoid contamination.

These are only some of the common things to follow especially for starters. Do not allow other pets to come near your garden and always check their condition. Most importantly, do not hesitate to ask if there are things not clear to you regarding hydroponic gardening.

Why Farming of the Future

Hydroponics gardening is indeed, offering a myriad of benefits not only for its growers but also for the human race. Nowadays, fresh water and adequate and healthy soil where we can plant and grow trees, fruits, herbs and veggies are becoming scarce. Whilst there are still important things to improve in this method, many still believe that with proper advancements and vast improvements, hydroponics can produce more quality by-products compared to traditional gardening. By using these hydroponic systems, we will be able to conserve water by consuming less of it without damaging or stunning the plant's growth.

Conclusion

Thank you again for downloading this book!

I hope this book was able to help you to have a deeper understanding of the hydroponic gardening and the systems to use.

The next step is to make your own hydroponic system at home and start growing plants hydroponically. Begin with small plants which are easier to grow and find yourself cultivating complex plants in the future! Do some research on the recent updates and innovation regarding this method and be able to share the knowledge, tips and strategies with your friends and family.

Remember, your tools and other needed materials do not have to be pricey. Follow the steps in lighting, proper feeding, cleaning and changing of nutrient solution to make the most out of your system.

Hydroponics gardening is a great way of growing your own plants especially if you are living in a high-rise building or renting a condo without the presence of fresh plants, fruit or veggies around. This method is also considered a great way to produce food in the future where soil gardening is not as effective and yielding as it was decades ago.

Likewise, other benefits such as relaxation, soothing effects, being one with nature and a perfect de-stressing hobby are what most growers enjoy in hydroponics gardening. You too, can experience all of this over time.

Finally, if you enjoyed this book, please take the time to share your thoughts and post a review on Amazon. It'd be greatly appreciated!

Thank you and good luck!

Printed in Poland
by Amazon Fulfillment
Poland Sp. z o.o., Wrocław